HOW LOVELY THE RUINS

HOW
LOVELY
THE RUINS

Inspirational Poems and Words
for Difficult Times

FOREWORD BY
ELIZABETH
ALEXANDER

SPIEGEL & GRAU
New York

Published in the United States by Spiegel & Grau, an imprint of
Random House, a division of Penguin Random House LLC, New York.

SPIEGEL & GRAU and Design is a registered trademark of
Penguin Random House LLC.

Permissions acknowledgments can be found starting on page 193.

LIBRARY OF CONGRESS CATALOGING-IN-PUBLICATION DATA
Names: Alexander, Elizabeth, writer of foreword.
Title: How lovely the ruins: inspirational poems and words for difficult
times / foreword by Elizabeth Alexander.
Description: First edition. | New York: Spiegel & Grau, 2017.
Identifiers: LCCN 2017035295 | ISBN 9780399592836
(hardback: acid-free paper) | ISBN 9780399592850 (ebook)
Subjects: LCSH: Inspiration—Literary collections. | Inspiration—Poetry.
| BISAC: POETRY / Anthologies (multiple authors). | POETRY /
Inspirational & Religious. | POETRY / General.
Classification: LCC PN6071.16 H69 2017 | DDC 808.8/0353—dc23
LC record available at https://lccn.loc.gov/2017035295

Printed in the United States of America on acid-free paper

randomhousebooks.com
spiegelandgrau.com

2 4 6 8 9 7 5 3 1

FIRST EDITION

TITLE-SPREAD IMAGE: iStock/catscandotcom

Book design by Simon M. Sullivan

I REFUSE TO ACCEPT THIS. I believe that man will not merely endure: he will prevail. He is immortal, not because he alone among creatures has an inexhaustible voice, but because he has a soul, a spirit capable of compassion and sacrifice and endurance. The poet's, the writer's, duty is to write about these things. It is his privilege to help man endure by lifting his heart, by reminding him of the courage and honor and hope and pride and compassion and pity and sacrifice which have been the glory of his past. The poet's voice need not merely be the record of man, it can be one of the props, the pillars to help him endure and prevail.

—WILLIAM FAULKNER,
Nobel lecture, December 10, 1950

CONTENTS

II. AGAINST TYRANNY

III. THE ACHING

IV. THE NEW PATRIOTS

V. GATHERING STRENGTH

VI. TO SUMMON HOPE

INTRODUCTION

===

IN THE LAST YEAR, we've noticed poetry filling our social media feeds as it never has before. Nearly each day, our friends and family members continue to post empowering and moving words—words that make us take notice, that give meaning to this moment we are living through, even as they speak out across time. The voices of Rumi, Langston Hughes, Emily Dickinson, and Danez Smith are bringing a new wind of hope, vigor, and clarity to a complex and tumultuous world.

Poetry is reverberating across the divide. Across all divides, in fact: the political divide, the economic divide, the gender divide, the generational divide. And even across the divides within ourselves: the hopeful and the hopeless; the engaged citizen and the parts of ourselves that feel numbed by the hypocrisy and injustice around us. A good poem speaks to us both individually and collectively. It expands our understanding of the world, challenges us, and can renew our faith in ourselves and in life in general. Sometimes we can come to know ourselves best and most intimately through poetry. And so we decided to create a collection to offer readers inspiration in these times of turmoil and divisiveness (and beyond). We collected poems we saw on Facebook. We turned to friends and colleagues for the poems that most spoke to them when nothing else seemed to help.

So here, for you to read in trying times both personal and universal, are words that guided us when we were full of doubt, gave us a sense of truth when it seemed remarkably hard to discern, reaffirmed our sense of ourselves when we felt lost, challenged us to see the world through others' eyes, comforted us when we despaired, created a sense of community when we felt alone, and filled us with faith when we felt on the verge of giving up.

May they light your path too.

ANNIE CHAGNOT and EMI IKKANDA
Spiegel & Grau editors

FOREWORD
Elizabeth Alexander

===

H UMAN BEINGS HAVE NEVER LIVED without song, across time and tribe. So poetry has always been necessary, and people have always made it, and shared it, and in some way lived by it. That is steady-state in human history. When language is degraded from the highest perches, and public words regularly carry meaning that reduces groups to crude and false stereotypes, the nuance and precision of poems is an ever more necessary tool for living.

Poems are how we say: *this is who we are*. Poems are heart and soul made legible. Poetry is ancient; poetry is the way peoples have carried their songs forward across culture and across time, saying this is who we are and this is where and what we come from.

This human will to sing is itself cross-cultural and cross-temporal. The will to sing is perhaps even biological, for who can imagine a child who does not sing, who does not urge to tell a story or sit riveted in the presence of one? This is the bardic aspect of poetry, the singing of the song of the people that is the work that poets do, even when there is no explicit "we" in the poem, even when the claims are not grand, even when the language is abstract. Poems are where voices can join together and sing in a voice more powerful than one. Poems mark a trail of identities; poems laid end to end are a map of the human voice.

The poems gathered in this volume move across time and place to remind us that the world has always been broken and has always been whole. The poem can potentially last forever and thus the poem outlasts the poet. For none of us individually will be able to tell our story for all time. Human beings have been vulnerable for as long as there have been human beings, some more so than others. As a student and caretaker of the tradition of black female creativity, I know that tradition has always given handbooks for hard times. So, too, the poems here. *Conduct your blooming in the noise and whip of the whirlwind,* wrote Gwendolyn Brooks, words that are always apt. I find that black elders offer the long view in ancestral hum: *make a way out of no way,* as they say. That genius.

The wisdom and beauty of poems is all around us. Poets tilt their heads and swoop their butterfly nets to capture it, distill it, and give it to the people. Poems are handbooks for human decency and understanding. Poets hold water in their cupped hands and run back from the well because someone is parched and thirsting. The poem is a force field against despair.

Sometimes, when times are tough, we may think we have nothing when we actually have everything. Because we are the survivors, and in these words we have all the ancestors have given us. Poems let us feel that power open up inside our bodies when we read the words out loud.

If the poems in this book had one voice chanting a refrain it would be: *My people, we have everything we need.*

May 2017
New York City

I

HOW LOVELY
THE RUINS

Try to Praise the Mutilated World

Adam Zagajewski

TRANSLATED BY CLARE CAVANAGH

Try to praise the mutilated world.
Remember June's long days,
and wild strawberries, drops of rosé wine.
The nettles that methodically overgrow
the abandoned homesteads of exiles.
You must praise the mutilated world.
You watched the stylish yachts and ships;
one of them had a long trip ahead of it,
while salty oblivion awaited others.
You've seen the refugees going nowhere,
you've heard the executioners sing joyfully.
You should praise the mutilated world.
Remember the moments when we were together
in a white room and the curtain fluttered.
Return in thought to the concert where music flared.
You gathered acorns in the park in autumn
and leaves eddied over the earth's scars.
Praise the mutilated world
and the gray feather a thrush lost,
and the gentle light that strays and vanishes
and returns.

THERE ARE BIRDS HERE
Jamaal May

For Detroit
There are birds here,
so many birds here
is what I was trying to say
when they said those birds were metaphors
for what is trapped
between buildings
and buildings. No.
The birds are here
to root around for bread
the girl's hands tear
and toss like confetti. No,
I don't mean the bread is torn like cotton,
I said confetti, and no
not the confetti
a tank can make of a building.
I mean the confetti
a boy can't stop smiling about
and no his smile isn't much
like a skeleton at all. And no
his neighborhood is not like a war zone.
I am trying to say
his neighborhood
is as tattered and feathered
as anything else,
as shadow pierced by sun
and light parted

by shadow-dance as anything else,
but they won't stop saying
how lovely the ruins,
how ruined the lovely
children must be in that birdless city.

"The Rubaiyat of Omar Khayyam"
Omar Khayyam

"When you are so full of sorrow
that you can't walk, can't cry anymore,
think about the green foliage that sparkles after
the rain. When the daylight exhausts you, when
you hope a final night will cover the world,
think about the awakening of a young child."

POEM
Muriel Rukeyser

I lived in the first century of world wars.
Most mornings I would be more or less insane,
The newspapers would arrive with their careless stories,
The news would pour out of various devices
Interrupted by attempts to sell products to the unseen.
I would call my friends on other devices;
They would be more or less mad for similar reasons.
Slowly I would get to pen and paper,
Make my poems for others unseen and unborn.
In the day I would be reminded of those men and women,
Brave, setting up signals across vast distances,
Considering a nameless way of living, of almost unimagined
    values.
As the lights darkened, as the lights of night brightened,
We would try to imagine them, try to find each other,
To construct peace, to make love, to reconcile
Waking with sleeping, ourselves with each other,
Ourselves with ourselves. We would try by any means
To reach the limits of ourselves, to reach beyond ourselves,
To let go the means, to wake.

I lived in the first century of these wars.

It's not that the stars
are indifferent: their troubles
have already passed

—CLARK STRAND

Fire and Ice
Robert Frost

Some say the world will end in fire,
Some say in ice.
From what I've tasted of desire
I hold with those who favor fire.
But if it had to perish twice,
I think I know enough of hate
To know that for destruction ice
Is also great
And would suffice.

THE PLACE WHERE WE ARE RIGHT

Yehuda Amichai

TRANSLATED BY CHANA BLOCH AND STEPHEN MITCHELL

From the place where we are right
Flowers will never grow
In the spring.

The place where we are right
Is hard and trampled
Like a yard.

But doubts and loves
Dig up the world
Like a mole, a plow.
And a whisper will be heard in the place
Where the ruined
House once stood.

ALL YOU WHO SLEEP TONIGHT
Vikram Seth

All you who sleep tonight
Far from the ones you love,
No hand to left or right,
And emptiness above—

Know that you aren't alone.
The whole world shares your tears,
Some for two nights or one,
And some for all their years.

The Guest House

Rumi

TRANSLATED BY COLEMAN BARKS

This being human is a guest house.
Every morning a new arrival.

A joy, a depression, a meanness,
some momentary awareness comes
As an unexpected visitor.

Welcome and entertain them all!
Even if they're a crowd of sorrows,
who violently sweep your house
empty of its furniture,
still treat each guest honorably.
He may be clearing you out
for some new delight.

The dark thought, the shame, the malice,
meet them at the door laughing,
and invite them in.

Be grateful for whoever comes,
because each has been sent
as a guide from beyond.

FROM
"THE SENTENCE"
Anna Akhmatova
TRANSLATED BY JUDITH HEMSCHEMEYER

Today I have so much to do:
I must kill memory once and for all,
I must turn my soul to stone,
I must learn to live again—

A Green Crab's Shell

Mark Doty

Not, exactly, green:
closer to bronze
preserved in kind brine,

something retrieved
from a Greco-Roman wreck,
patinated and oddly

muscular. We cannot
know what his fantastic
legs were like—

though evidence
suggests eight
complexly folded

scuttling works
of armament, crowned
by the foreclaws'

gesture of menace
and power. A gull's
gobbled the center,

leaving this chamber
—size of a demitasse—
open to reveal

a shocking, Giotto blue.
Though it smells
of seaweed and ruin,

this little traveling case
comes with such lavish lining!
Imagine breathing

surrounded by
the brilliant rinse
of summer's firmament.

What color is
the underside of skin?
Not so bad, to die,

if we could be opened
into *this*—
if the smallest chambers

of ourselves,
similarly,
revealed some sky.

DOVER BEACH
Matthew Arnold

The sea is calm tonight.
The tide is full, the moon lies fair
Upon the straits; on the French coast the light
Gleams and is gone; the cliffs of England stand,
Glimmering and vast, out in the tranquil bay.
Come to the window, sweet is the night-air!
Only, from the long line of spray
Where the sea meets the moon-blanched land,
Listen! you hear the grating roar
Of pebbles which the waves draw back, and fling,
At their return, up the high strand,
Begin, and cease, and then again begin,
With tremulous cadence slow, and bring
The eternal note of sadness in.

Sophocles long ago
Heard it on the Ægean, and it brought
Into his mind the turbid ebb and flow
Of human misery; we
Find also in the sound a thought,
Hearing it by this distant northern sea.

The Sea of Faith
Was once, too, at the full, and round earth's shore
Lay like the folds of a bright girdle furled.
But now I only hear
Its melancholy, long, withdrawing roar,

Retreating, to the breath
Of the night-wind, down the vast edges drear
And naked shingles of the world.

Ah, love, let us be true
To one another! for the world, which seems
To lie before us like a land of dreams,
So various, so beautiful, so new,
Hath really neither joy, nor love, nor light,
Nor certitude, nor peace, nor help for pain;
And we are here as on a darkling plain
Swept with confused alarms of struggle and flight,
Where ignorant armies clash by night.

Out Beyond Ideas

Rumi

TRANSLATED BY COLEMAN BARKS

Out beyond ideas of wrongdoing and rightdoing,
there is a field. I'll meet you there.

When the soul lies down in that grass,
the world is too full to talk about.
Ideas, language, even the phrase *each other*
doesn't make any sense.

Barn's burnt down—
now
I can see the moon.

—MASAHIDE

What Kind of Times Are These
Adrienne Rich

There's a place between two stands of trees where the grass
    grows uphill
and the old revolutionary road breaks off into shadows
near a meeting-house abandoned by the persecuted
who disappeared into those shadows.

I've walked there picking mushrooms at the edge of dread, but
    don't be fooled,
this isn't a Russian poem, this is not somewhere else but here,
our country moving closer to its own truth and dread,
its own ways of making people disappear.

I won't tell you where the place is, the dark mesh of the woods
meeting the unmarked strip of light—
ghost-ridden crossroads, leafmold paradise:
I know already who wants to buy it, sell it, make it disappear.

And I won't tell you where it is, so why do I tell you
anything? Because you still listen, because in times like these
to have you listen at all, it's necessary
to talk about trees.

Musée des Beaux Arts
W. H. *Auden*

About suffering they were never wrong,
The old Masters: how well they understood
Its human position: how it takes place
While someone else is eating or opening a window or just
    walking dully along;
How, when the aged are reverently, passionately waiting
For the miraculous birth, there always must be
Children who did not specially want it to happen, skating
On a pond at the edge of the wood:
They never forgot
That even the dreadful martyrdom must run its course
Anyhow in a corner, some untidy spot
Where the dogs go on with their doggy life and the torturer's
    horse
Scratches its innocent behind on a tree.

In Breughel's *Icarus*, for instance: how everything turns away
Quite leisurely from the disaster; the ploughman may
Have heard the splash, the forsaken cry,
But for him it was not an important failure; the sun shone
As it had to on the white legs disappearing into the green
Water, and the expensive delicate ship that must have seen
Something amazing, a boy falling out of the sky,
Had somewhere to get to and sailed calmly on.

When you consider things like the stars, our affairs
don't seem to matter very much, do they?

—VIRGINIA WOOLF

SCI-FI
Tracy K. Smith

There will be no edges, but curves.
Clean lines pointing only forward.

History, with its hard spine & dog-eared
Corners, will be replaced with nuance,

Just like the dinosaurs gave way
To mounds and mounds of ice.

Women will still be women, but
The distinction will be empty. Sex,

Having outlived every threat, will gratify
Only the mind, which is where it will exist.

For kicks, we'll dance for ourselves
Before mirrors studded with golden bulbs.

The oldest among us will recognize that glow—
But the word *sun* will have been re-assigned

To the Standard Uranium-Neutralizing device
Found in households and nursing homes.

And yes, we'll live to be much older, thanks
To popular consensus. Weightless, unhinged,

Eons from even our own moon, we'll drift
In the haze of space, which will be, once

And for all, scrutable and safe.

II

AGAINST
TYRANNY

One's philosophy is not best expressed in words; it is expressed in the choices one makes. In stopping to think through the meaning of what I have learned, there is much that I believe intensely, much I am unsure of. In the long run, we shape our lives and we shape ourselves. The process never ends until we die. And, the choices we make are ultimately our own responsibility.

—ELEANOR ROOSEVELT

"Nineteen Hundred and Nineteen"
W. B. Yeats

We too had many pretty toys when young:
A law indifferent to blame or praise,
To bribe or threat; habits that made old wrong
Melt down, as it were wax in the sun's rays;
Public opinion ripening for so long
We thought it would outlive all future days.
O what fine thought we had because we thought
That the worst rogues and rascals had died out. . . .

I Hear America Singing

Walt Whitman

I hear America singing, the varied carols I hear,
Those of mechanics, each one singing his as it should be blithe
    and strong,
The carpenter singing his as he measures his plank or beam,
The mason singing his as he makes ready for work, or leaves off
    work,
The boatman singing what belongs to him in his boat, the
    deckhand singing on the steamboat deck,
The shoemaker singing as he sits on his bench, the hatter singing
    as he stands,
The wood-cutter's song, the ploughboy's on his way in the
    morning, or at noon intermission or at sundown,
The delicious singing of the mother, or of the young wife at
    work, or of the girl sewing or washing,
Each singing what belongs to him or her and to none else,
The day what belongs to the day—at night the party of young
    fellows, robust, friendly,
Singing with open mouths their strong melodious songs.

DIFFERENCES OF OPINION

Wendy Cope

I

HE TELLS HER

He tells her that the earth is flat—
He knows the facts, and that is that.
In altercations fierce and long
She tries her best to prove him wrong.
But he has learned to argue well.
He calls her arguments unsound
And often asks her not to yell.
She cannot win. He stands his ground.

The planet goes on being round.

TERENCE, THIS IS STUPID STUFF

A. E. Housman

'Terence, this is stupid stuff:
You eat your victuals fast enough;
There can't be much amiss, 'tis clear,
To see the rate you drink your beer.
But oh, good Lord, the verse you make,
It gives a chap the belly-ache.
The cow, the old cow, she is dead;
It sleeps well, the horned head:
We poor lads, 'tis our turn now
To hear such tunes as killed the cow.
Pretty friendship 'tis to rhyme
Your friends to death before their time
Moping melancholy mad:
Come, pipe a tune to dance to, lad.'

Why, if 'tis dancing you would be,
There's brisker pipes than poetry.
Say, for what were hop-yards meant,
Or why was Burton built on Trent?
Oh many a peer of England brews
Livelier liquor than the Muse,
And malt does more than Milton can
To justify God's ways to man.
Ale, man, ale's the stuff to drink
For fellows whom it hurts to think:
Look into the pewter pot
To see the world as the world's not.
And faith, 'tis pleasant till 'tis past:

The mischief is that 'twill not last.
Oh I have been to Ludlow fair
And left my necktie God knows where,
And carried half way home, or near,
Pints and quarts of Ludlow beer:
Then the world seemed none so bad,
And I myself a sterling lad;
And down in lovely muck I've lain,
Happy till I woke again.
Then I saw the morning sky:
Heigho, the tale was all a lie;
The world, it was the old world yet,
I was I, my things were wet,
And nothing now remained to do
But begin the game anew.

Therefore, since the world has still
Much good, but much less good than ill,
And while the sun and moon endure
Luck's a chance, but trouble's sure,
I'd face it as a wise man would,
And train for ill and not for good.
'Tis true, the stuff I bring for sale
Is not so brisk a brew as ale:
Out of a stem that scored the hand
I wrung it in a weary land.
But take it: if the smack is sour,
The better for the embittered hour;
It should do good to heart and head
When your soul is in my soul's stead;
And I will friend you, if I may,
In the dark and cloudy day.

There was a king reigned in the East:
There, when kings will sit to feast,
They get their fill before they think
With poisoned meat and poisoned drink.
He gathered all that springs to birth
From the many-venomed earth;
First a little, thence to more,
He sampled all her killing store;
And easy, smiling, seasoned sound,
Sate the king when healths went round.
They put arsenic in his meat
And stared aghast to watch him eat;
They poured strychnine in his cup
And shook to see him drink it up:
They shook, they stared as white's their shirt:
Them it was their poison hurt.
—I tell the tale that I heard told.
Mithridates, he died old.

To say that the future will be different from the present is, to scientists, hopelessly self-evident. I observe regretfully that in politics, however, it can be heresy. It can be denounced as radicalism, or branded as subversion. There are people in every time and every land who want to stop history in its tracks. They fear the future, mistrust the present, and invoke the security of a comfortable past which, in fact, never existed.

—ROBERT F. KENNEDY

PROTEST
Ella Wheeler Wilcox

To sin by silence, when we should protest,
Makes cowards out of men. The human race
Has climbed on protest. Had no voice been raised
Against injustice, ignorance, and lust,
The inquisition yet would serve the law,
And guillotines decide our least disputes.
The few who dare, must speak and speak again
To right the wrongs of many. Speech, thank God,
No vested power in this great day and land
Can gag or throttle. Press and voice may cry
Loud disapproval of existing ills;
May criticise oppression and condemn
The lawlessness of wealth-protecting laws
That let the children and childbearers toil
To purchase ease for idle millionaires.

Therefore I do protest against the boast
Of independence in this mighty land.
Call no chain strong, which holds one rusted link.
Call no land free, that holds one fettered slave.
Until the manacled slim wrists of babes
Are loosed to toss in childish sport and glee,
Until the mother bears no burden, save
The precious one beneath her heart, until
God's soil is rescued from the clutch of greed
And given back to labor, let no man
Call this the land of freedom.

Choose your leaders with wisdom and forethought.
To be led by a coward is to be controlled by all that the coward
fears.
To be led by a fool is to be led by the opportunists who control
the fool.
To be led by a thief is to offer up your most precious treasures to
be stolen.
To be led by a liar is to ask to be told lies.
To be led by a tyrant is to sell yourself and those you love into
slavery.

—OCTAVIA E. BUTLER, *Parable of the Talents*

WHAT IT LOOK LIKE
Terrance Hayes

Dear Ol' Dirty Bastard: I too like it raw,
I don't especially care for Duke Ellington
at a birthday party. I care less and less
about the shapes of shapes because forms
change and nothing is more durable than feeling.
My uncle used the money I gave him
to buy a few vials of what looked like candy
after the party where my grandma sang
in an outfit that was obviously made
for a West African king. My motto is
Never mistake what it is for what it looks like.
My generosity, for example, is mostly a form
of vanity. A bandanna is a useful handkerchief,
but a handkerchief is a useless-ass bandanna.
This only looks like a footnote in my report
concerning the party. *Trill* stands for what is
truly real though it may be hidden by the houses
just over the hills between us, by the hands
on the bars between us. That picture
of my grandmother with my uncle
when he was a baby is not trill. What it is
is the feeling felt seeing garbagemen drift
along the predawn avenues, a sloppy slow rain
taking its time to the coast. Milquetoast
is not trill, nor is bouillabaisse. *Bakku-shan*
is Japanese for a woman who is beautiful
only when viewed from behind. Like I was saying,
my motto is *Never mistake what it looks like*

for what it is else you end up like that Negro
Othello. (Was Othello a Negro?) Don't you lie
about who you are sometimes and then realize
the lie is true? You are blind to your power, Brother
Bastard, like the king who wanders his kingdom
searching for the king. And that's okay.
No one will tell you you are the king.
No one really wants a king anyway.

ELECTION
John Holmes

Cezanne, when he was old, shouted in the streets,
"This world is wild with horrors and with hates."

"The world, the world," Rilke wrote in Munich long ago,
"Has lost all those old men who would weep now,

Weep before the peoples, prophets having that power."
Innocent Einstein asked how so many could not care,

And so much wrong. MacNeice said, in Dublin later,
Being a poet too, and young, "The world is crazier

And more of it than we think." You by ballot praise
An old whoring dishonest drinking ruthless easy

Image of statesmanship, over and over again,
Lined up at the polls with bitter but not better men.

Hope is definitely not the same thing as optimism. It is not the conviction that something will turn out well, but the certainty that something makes sense, regardless of how it turns out.

—Václav Havel

VIEWERS MAY THINK THAT THEY
CAN PROCESS IT ALL
Stephanie Gray

but they are fooling themselves, if there's a window open you
might have a chance, if you hadn't all gone to Holy Name, if the
world didn't change, if you only bent the laws of physics so
much, if the tides weren't so strong on the Hudson, if you didn't
have to go, if it wasn't a dream you still believed in, if that
different kind of memory didn't take hold, if your muscle
memory didn't steady you, if you didn't have orders you couldn't
ship, if you didn't see what you saw, if the crawl wasn't always
hungry, if there weren't celebrities in every sphere, if you didn't
know all the criminals in the neighborhood, if nothing ever
happened here, if it wasn't a country club, if there wasn't magic
in actuality, if you didn't dislocate the phrase, if you didn't grind
the blue sky, if it hadn't been a downward trajectory, if the
shadow didn't undo itself, if you all weren't all on break, if
everyone didn't shut down, if Canada wasn't in the escape plans,
if the future wasn't sparkling with nostalgia

EXPERIENCE
Carl Sandburg

This morning I looked at the map of the day
And said to myself, "This is the way! This is the way I will go;
Thus shall I range on the roads of achievement,
The way is so clear—it shall all be a joy on the lines marked out."
And then as I went came a place that was strange,—
'Twas a place not down on the map!
And I stumbled and fell and lay in the weeds,
And looked on the day with rue.

I am learning a little—never to be sure—
To be positive only with what is past,
And to peer sometimes at the things to come
As a wanderer treading the night
When the mazy stars neither point nor beckon,
And of all the roads, no road is sure.

I see those men with maps and talk
Who tell how to go and where and why;
I hear with my ears the words of their mouths,
As they finger with ease the marks on the maps;
And only as one looks robust, lonely, and querulous,
As if he had gone to a country far
And made for himself a map,
Do I cry to him, "I would see your map!
I would heed that map you have!"

Global Warming
Jane Hirshfield

When his ship first came to Australia,
Cook wrote, the natives
continued fishing, without looking up.
Unable, it seems, to fear what was too large to be comprehended.

September 1, 1939
W. H. Auden

I sit in one of the dives
On Fifty-second Street
Uncertain and afraid
As the clever hopes expire
Of a low dishonest decade:
Waves of anger and fear
Circulate over the bright
And darkened lands of the earth,
Obsessing our private lives;
The unmentionable odour of death
Offends the September night.

Accurate scholarship can
Unearth the whole offence
From Luther until now
That has driven a culture mad,
Find what occurred at Linz,
What huge imago made
A psychopathic god:
I and the public know
What all schoolchildren learn,
Those to whom evil is done
Do evil in return.

Exiled Thucydides knew
All that a speech can say
About Democracy,
And what dictators do,

The elderly rubbish they talk
To an apathetic grave;
Analysed all in his book,
The enlightenment driven away,
The habit-forming pain,
Mismanagement and grief:
We must suffer them all again.

Into this neutral air
Where blind skyscrapers use
Their full height to proclaim
The strength of Collective Man,
Each language pours its vain
Competitive excuse:
But who can live for long
In an euphoric dream;
Out of the mirror they stare,
Imperialism's face
And the international wrong.

Faces along the bar
Cling to their average day:
The lights must never go out,
The music must always play,
All the conventions conspire
To make this fort assume
The furniture of home;
Lest we should see where we are,
Lost in a haunted wood,
Children afraid of the night
Who have never been happy or good.

The windiest militant trash
Important Persons shout
Is not so crude as our wish:
What mad Nijinsky wrote
About Diaghilev
Is true of the normal heart;
For the error bred in the bone
Of each woman and each man
Craves what it cannot have,
Not universal love
But to be loved alone.

From the conservative dark
Into the ethical life
The dense commuters come,
Repeating their morning vow;
'I will be true to the wife,
I'll concentrate more on my work,'
And helpless governors wake
To resume their compulsory game:
Who can release them now,
Who can reach the deaf,
Who can speak for the dumb?

All I have is a voice
To undo the folded lie,
The romantic lie in the brain
Of the sensual man-in-the-street
And the lie of Authority
Whose buildings grope the sky:
There is no such thing as the State
And no one exists alone;

Hunger allows no choice
To the citizen or the police;
We must love one another or die.

Defenseless under the night
Our world in stupor lies;
Yet, dotted everywhere,
Ironic points of light
Flash out wherever the Just
Exchange their messages:
May I, composed like them
Of Eros and of dust,
Beleaguered by the same
Negation and despair,
Show an affirming flame.

EVIL
Langston Hughes

Looks like what drives me crazy
Don't have no effect on you—
But I'm gonna keep on at it
Till it drives you crazy, too.

AMERICAN PHAROAH
Ada Limón

Despite the morning's gray static of rain,
we drive to Churchill Downs at 6 a.m.,
eyes still swollen shut with sleep. I say,
Remember when I used to think everything
was getting better and better? Now, I think
it's just getting worse and worse. I know it's not
what I'm supposed to say as we machine our
way through the silent seventy minutes on 64
over pavement still fractured from the winter's
wreckage. I'm tired. I've had vertigo for five
months and on my first day home, he's shaken
me awake to see this horse, not even race, but
work. He gives me his jacket as we face
the deluge from car to the twin spire turnstiles,
and once deep in the fern-green grandstands, I see
the crowd. A few hundred maybe, black umbrellas,
cameras, and notepads, wet-winged eager early birds
come to see this Kentucky-bred bay colt with his
chewed-off tail train to end the almost 40-year
American Triple Crown drought. A man next to us,
some horseracing heavy, ticks off a list of reasons
why this horse—his speed-laden pedigree, muscle
and bone recovery, et cetera, et cetera—could never
win the grueling mile-and-a-half Belmont Stakes.
Then, the horse with his misspelled name comes out,
first just casually cantering with his lead horse,
and next, a brief break in the storm, and he's racing
against no one but himself and the official clocker,

monstrously fast and head down so we can see
that faded star flash on his forehead like this
is real gladness. As the horse eases up and we
close our mouths to swallow, the heavy next to us
folds his arms, says what I want to say too: *I take it all back.*

He held the Beast of the Apocalypse by its tail, the stupid kid! Oh beards on fire, our doom appeared sealed. The buildings were tottering; the computer screens were as dark as our grandmother's cupboards. We were too frightened to plead. Another century gone to hell—and for what? Just because some people don't know how to bring their children up!

—CHARLES SIMIC

"To a Friend Whose Work Has Come to Nothing"

W. B. Yeats

Now all the truth is out,
Be secret and take defeat
From any brazen throat,
For how can you compete,
Being honor bred, with one
Who were it proved he lies
Were neither shamed in his own
Nor in his neighbours' eyes. . . .

"TOWARD NIGHTFALL"

FOR DON AND JANE

Charles Simic

The weight of tragic events
On everyone's back,
Just as tragedy
In the proper Greek sense
Was thought impossible
To compose in our day.

There were scaffolds,
Makeshift stages,
Puny figures on them,
Like small indistinct animals
Caught in the headlights
Crossing the road way ahead . . .

. . . It's just a bad chill,
She keeps telling herself
Not having seen the papers
Which the landlord has the dog
Bring from the front porch.

The old man never learned
To read well, and so
Reads on in that half-whisper,
And in that half-light
Verging on the dark,

About that day's tragedies
Which supposedly are not
Tragedies in the absence of
Figures endowed with
Classic nobility of soul.

If it is not tempered by compassion and empathy, reason can lead men and women into a moral void.

—KAREN ARMSTRONG

I Work All Day . . .

Pier Paolo Pasolini

TRANSLATED BY LAWRENCE FERLINGHETTI
AND FRANCESCA VALENTE

I work all day like a monk
and at night wander about like an alleycat
looking for love . . . I'll propose
to the Church that I be made a saint.
In fact I respond to mystification
with mildness. I watch the lynch-mob
as through a camera-eye.
With the calm and courage of a scientist,
I watch myself being massacred.
I seem to feel hate and yet I write
verses of painstaking love.
I study treachery as a fatal phenomenon,
almost as if I were not its object.
I pity the young fascists,
and the old ones, whom I consider forms
of the most horrible evil, I oppose
only with the violence of reason.
Passive as a bird that sees all, in flight,
carries in its heart,
rising in the sky,
an unforgiving conscience.

Preparation
Effie Waller Smith

"I have no time for those things now," we say;
"But in the future just a little way,
 No longer by this ceaseless toil oppressed,
 I shall have leisure then for thought and rest.
 When I the debts upon my land have paid,
 Or on foundations firm my business laid,
 I shall take time for discourse long and sweet
 With those beloved who round my hearthstone meet;
 I shall take time on mornings still and cool
 To seek the freshness dim of wood and pool,
 Where, calmed and hallowed by great Nature's peace,
 My life from its hot cares shall find release;
 I shall take time to think on destiny,
 Of what I was and am and yet shall be,
 Till in the hush my soul may nearer prove
 To that great Soul in whom we live and move.
 All this I shall do sometime but not now—
 The press of business cares will not allow."
 And thus our life glides on year after year;
 The promised leisure never comes more near.
 Perhaps the aim on which we placed our mind
 Is high, and its attainment slow to find;
 Or if we reach the mark that we have set,
 We still would seek another, farther yet.
 Thus all our youth, our strength, our time go past
 Till death upon the threshold stands at last,
 And back unto our Maker we must give
 The life we spent preparing well to live.

III

THE
ACHING

That's the thing about pain, it demands to be felt.

—JOHN GREEN, *The Fault in Our Stars*

AMERICA

Claude McKay

Although she feeds me bread of bitterness,
And sinks into my throat her tiger's tooth,
Stealing my breath of life, I will confess
I love this cultured hell that tests my youth!
Her vigor flows like tides into my blood,
Giving me strength erect against her hate.
Her bigness sweeps my being like a flood.
Yet as a rebel fronts a king in state,
I stand within her walls with not a shred
Of terror, malice, not a word of jeer.
Darkly I gaze into the days ahead,
And see her might and granite wonders there,
Beneath the touch of Time's unerring hand,
Like priceless treasures sinking in the sand.

Remember
Christina Rossetti

Remember me when I am gone away,
    Gone far away into the silent land;
    When you can no more hold me by the hand,
Nor I half turn to go yet turning stay.
Remember me when no more day by day
    You tell me of our future that you planned:
    Only remember me; you understand
It will be late to counsel then or pray.
Yet if you should forget me for a while
    And afterwards remember, do not grieve:
    For if the darkness and corruption leave
A vestige of the thoughts that once I had,
Better by far you should forget and smile
    Than that you should remember and be sad.

GOOD BONES
Maggie Smith

Life is short, though I keep this from my children.
Life is short, and I've shortened mine
in a thousand delicious, ill-advised ways,
a thousand deliciously ill-advised ways
I'll keep from my children. The world is at least
fifty percent terrible, and that's a conservative
estimate, though I keep this from my children.
For every bird there is a stone thrown at a bird.
For every loved child, a child broken, bagged,
sunk in a lake. Life is short and the world
is at least half terrible, and for every kind
stranger, there is one who would break you,
though I keep this from my children. I am trying
to sell them the world. Any decent realtor,
walking you through a real shithole, chirps on
about good bones: This place could be beautiful,
right? You could make this place beautiful.

DIRGE WITHOUT MUSIC
Edna St. Vincent Millay

I am not resigned to the shutting away of loving hearts in the
hard ground.
So it is, and so it will be, for so it has been, time out of mind:
Into the darkness they go, the wise and the lovely. Crowned
With lilies and with laurel they go; but I am not resigned.

Lovers and thinkers, into the earth with you.
Be one with the dull, the indiscriminate dust.
A fragment of what you felt, of what you knew,
A formula, a phrase remains,—but the best is lost.

The answers quick and keen, the honest look, the laughter, the
love,—
They are gone. They are gone to feed the roses. Elegant and
curled
Is the blossom. Fragrant is the blossom. I know. But I do not
approve.
More precious was the light in your eyes than all the roses in the
world.

Down, down, down into the darkness of the grave
Gently they go, the beautiful, the tender, the kind;
Quietly they go, the intelligent, the witty, the brave.
I know. But I do not approve. And I am not resigned.

Four in the Morning
Wisława Szymborska

TRANSLATED BY MAGNUS J. KRYNSKI AND ROBERT A. MAGUIRE

The hour from night to day.
The hour from side to side.
The hour for those past thirty.

The hour swept clean to the crowing of cocks.
The hour when earth betrays us.
The hour when wind blows from extinguished stars.
The hour of and-what-if-nothing-remains-after-us.

The hollow hour.
Blank, empty.
The very pit of all other hours.

No one feels good at four in the morning.
If ants feel good at four in the morning
—three cheers for the ants. And let five o'clock come
if we're to go on living.

Life is to be lived, not controlled; and humanity is won by continuing to play in face of certain defeat.

—RALPH ELLISON, *Invisible Man*

CREDO

Edwin Arlington Robinson

I cannot find my way: there is no star
In all the shrouded heavens anywhere;
And there is not a whisper in the air
Of any living voice but one so far
That I can hear it only as a bar
Of lost, imperial music, played when fair
And angel fingers wove, and unawares,
Dead leaves to garlands where no roses are.

No, there is not a glimmer, nor a call,
For one that welcomes, welcomes when he fears,
The black and awful chaos of the night;
For through it all—above, beyond it all—
I know the far-sent message of the years,
I feel the coming glory of the Light.

Hours
Hazel Hall

I have known hours built like cities,
House on grey house, with streets between
That lead to straggling roads and trail off,
Forgotten in a field of green;

Hours made like mountains lifting
White crests out of the fog and rain,
And woven of forbidden music—
Hours eternal in their pain.

Life is a tapestry of hours
Forever mellowing in tone,
Where all things blend, even the longing
For hours I have never known.

The Thing Is

Ellen Bass

to love life, to love it even
when you have no stomach for it
and everything you've held dear
crumbles like burnt paper in your hands,
your throat filled with the silt of it.
When grief sits with you, its tropical heat
thickening the air, heavy as water
more fit for gills than lungs;
when grief weights you like your own flesh
only more of it, an obesity of grief,
you think, *How can a body withstand this?*
Then you hold life like a face
between your palms, a plain face,
no charming smile, no violet eyes,
and you say, yes, I will take you
I will love you, again.

IF I CAN STOP ONE HEART FROM BREAKING
Emily Dickinson

If I can stop one heart from breaking,
I shall not live in vain;
If I can ease one life the aching,
Or cool one pain,
Or help one fainting robin
Unto his nest again,
I shall not live in vain.

A Display of Mackerel

Mark Doty

They lie in parallel rows,
on ice, head to tail,
each a foot of luminosity

barred with black bands,
which divide the scales'
radiant sections

like seams of lead
in a Tiffany window.
Iridescent, watery

prismatics: think abalone,
the wildly rainbowed
mirror of a soapbubble sphere,

think sun on gasoline.
Splendor, and splendor,
and not a one in any way

distinguished from the other
—nothing about them
of individuality. Instead

they're *all* exact expressions
of the one soul,
each a perfect fulfilment

of heaven's template,
mackerel essence. As if,
after a lifetime arriving

at this enameling, the jeweler's
made uncountable examples,
each as intricate

in its oily fabulation
as the one before.
Suppose we could iridesce,

like these, and lose ourselves
entirely in the universe
of shimmer—would you want

to be yourself only,
unduplicatable, doomed
to be lost? They'd prefer,

plainly, to be flashing participants,
multitudinous. Even now
they seem to be bolting

forward, heedless of stasis.
They don't care they're dead
and nearly frozen,

just as, presumably,
they didn't care that they were living:
all, all for all,

the rainbowed school
and its acres of brilliant classrooms,
in which no verb is singular,

or every one is. How happy they seem,
even on ice, to be together, selfless,
which is the price of gleaming.

A hundred times every day I remind myself that my inner and outer life are based on the labors of other men, living and dead, and that I must exert myself in order to give in the same measure as I have received and am still receiving.

—ALBERT EINSTEIN, *The World as I See It*

Q & A

Kenneth Fearing

Where analgesia may be found to ease the infinite, minute scars
of the day;
What final interlude will result, picked bit by bit from the
morning's hurry, the lunch-hour boredom, the fevers of the
night;
Why this one is cherished by the gods, and that one not;
How to win, and win again, and again, staking wit alone against a
sea of time;
Which man to trust and, once found, how far—

Will not be found in Matthew, Mark, Luke, or John,
Nor Blackstone, nor Gray's, nor Dun & Bradstreet, nor Freud,
nor Marx,
Nor the sage of the evening news, nor the corner astrologist, nor
in any poet,

Nor what sort of laughter should greet the paid pronouncements
of the great,
Nor what pleasure the multitudes have, bringing lunch and the
children to watch the condemned to be plunged into death,

Nor why the sun should rise tomorrow,
Nor how the moon still weaves upon the ground, through the
leaves, so much silence and so much peace.

HANDS
Safiya Sinclair

Out here the surf rewrites our silences.
This smell of ocean may never leave me;
our humble life or the sea a dark page

I am trying to turn: Today my mother's words
sound final. And perhaps this is her first true thing.
Her hands have not been her hands

since she was twelve,
motherless and shucking whatever the sea
could offer, each day orphaned in the tide

of her own necessity—where the men-o-war
ballooned, wearing her face, her anchor of a heart
reaching, mooring for any blasted thing:

sea-roach and black-haired kelp, jeweled perch
or a drop of pearl made with her smallest self,
her night-prayers a hushed word of thanks.

But out here the salt-depths refuse tragedy.
This hand-me-down life burns sufficiently tragic—
here what was cannibal masters the colonial

curse, carved our own language of the macabre,
sucking on the thumb of our own disparity. Holding
her spliff in the wind, she probes and squalls,

trying to remember the face of her own mother,
our island or some strange word she once found
amongst the filth of sailors whose beds she made,

whose shoes she shined, whose guns
she cleaned, while the white bullet of America
ricocheted in her brain. Still that face she can't recall

made her chew her fingernails, scratch the day down
to its blood, the rusty sunset of this wonder,
this smashed archipelago. Our wild sea-grape kingdom

overrun, gold and belonging in all its glory
to no one. How being twelve-fingered she took her father's
fishing line to the deviation, and starved

of blood what grew savage and unwanted. Pulled
until they shriveled away, two hungry mouths
askance and blooming, reminding her

that she was still woman always multiplying
as life's little nubs and dreams came bucking up
in her disjointed. How on the god-teeth

she cut this life, offered her hands and vessel
to be made wide, made purposeful,
her body opalescent with all our clamoring,

our bloodline of what once lived
and will live and live again.
In the sea's one voice she hears her answer.

Beneath her gravid belly
my gliding hull
a conger eel.

SOME YEARS THERE EXISTS
A WANTING TO ESCAPE—
Claudia Rankine

Some years there exists a wanting to escape—

you, floating above your certain ache—

still the ache coexists.

Call that the immanent you—

You are you even before you

grow into understanding you

are not anyone, worthless,

not worth you.

Even as your own weight insists

you are here, fighting off

the weight of nonexistence.

And still this life parts your lids, you see

you seeing your extending hand

as a falling wave—

/

I they he she we you turn

only to discover

the encounter

to be alien to this place.

Wait.

The patience is in the living. Time opens out to you.

The opening, between you and you, occupied,
zoned for an encounter,

given the histories of you and you—

And always, who is this you?

The start of you, each day,
a presence already—

Hey you—

/

Slipping down burying the you buried within. You are
everywhere and you are nowhere in the day.

The outside comes in—

Then you, hey you—

Overheard in the moonlight.

Overcome in the moonlight.

Soon you are sitting around, publicly listening, when you
hear this—what happens to you doesn't belong to you,
only half concerns you. He is speaking of the legionnaires
in Claire Denis's film *Beau Travail* and you are pulled back
into the body of you receiving the nothing gaze—

The world out there insisting on this only half concerns
you. What happens to you doesn't belong to you, only half
concerns you. It's not yours. Not yours only.

/

And still a world begins its furious erasure—
Who do you think you are, saying I to me?
You nothing.
You nobody.
You.

A body in the world drowns in it—
Hey you—

All our fevered history won't instill insight,
won't turn a body conscious,
won't make that look
in the eyes say yes, though there is nothing

to solve

even as each moment is an answer.

/

Don't say I if it means so little,
holds the little forming no one.
You are not sick, you are injured—

you ache for the rest of life.

How to care for the injured body,

the kind of body that can't hold
the content it is living?

And where is the safest place when that place
must be someplace other than in the body?

Even now your voice entangles this mouth
whose words are here as pulse, strumming
shut out, shut in, shut up—

You cannot say—

A body translates its you—

you there, hey you

/

even as it loses the location of its mouth.

When you lay your body in the body
entered as if skin and bone were public places,

when you lay your body in the body
entered as if you're the ground you walk on,

you know no memory should live
in these memories

becoming the body of you.

You slow all existence down with your call
detectable only as sky. The night's yawn
absorbs you as you lie down at the wrong angle

to the sun ready already to let go of your hand.

Wait with me
though the waiting, wait up,
might take until nothing whatsoever was done.

/

To be left, not alone, the only wish—

to call you out, to call out you.

Who shouted, you? You

shouted you, you the murmur in the air, you sometimes
sounding like you, you sometimes saying you,

go nowhere,

be no one but you first—

Nobody notices, only you've known,

you're not sick, not crazy,
not angry, not sad—

It's just this, you're injured.

/

Everything shaded everything darkened everything
shadowed

is the stripped is the struck—

is the trace
is the aftertaste.

I they he she we you were too concluded yesterday to know whatever was done could also be done, was also done, was never done—

The worst injury is feeling you don't belong so much to you—

The truth may be puzzling. It may take some work to grapple with. It may be counterintuitive. It may contradict deeply held prejudices. It may not be consonant with what we desperately want to be true. But our preferences do not determine what's true. We have a method, and that method helps us to reach not absolute truth, only asymptotic approaches to the truth—never there, just closer and closer, always finding vast new oceans of undiscovered possibilities.

—CARL SAGAN

It Comes in Every Storm
Olga Orozco
TRANSLATED BY MARY CROW

And don't you feel also, perhaps, a stormy sorrow on the skin of
 time,
like a scar that opens again
there where the sky was uprooted?
And don't you feel sometimes how that night gathers its tatters
 into an ominous bird,
that there's a beating of wings against the roof
like a clash among immense spring leaves struggling
or of hands clapping to summon you to death?
And don't you feel afterwards someone exiled is crying,
that there's an ember of a fallen angel on the threshold,
brought suddenly like a beggar by an alien gust of wind?
And don't you feel, like me, that a house rolling toward the abyss
runs over you with a crash of crockery shattered by lightning,
with two empty shells embracing each other for an endless journey,
with a screech of axles suddenly fractured like love's broken
 promises?
And don't you feel then your bed sinking like the nave of a
 cathedral crushed by the fall of heaven,
and that a thick, heavy water runs over your face till the final
 judgment?

Again it's the slime.
Again your heart thrown into the depth of the pool,
prisoner once more among the waves closing a dream.

Lie down as I do in this miserable eternity of one day.
It's useless to howl.
From these waters the beasts of oblivion don't drink.

"At a Window"
Carl Sandburg

Give me hunger,
O you gods that sit and give
The world its orders.
Give me hunger, pain and want,
Shut me out with shame and failure
From your doors of gold and fame,
Give me your shabbiest, weariest hunger!

GOD SPEAKS TO EACH OF US AS HE MAKES US

Rainer Maria Rilke

TRANSLATED BY ANITA BARROWS AND JOANNA MACY

God speaks to each of us as he makes us,
then walks with us silently out of the night.

These are the words we dimly hear:

You, sent out beyond your recall,
go to the limits of your longing.
Embody me.

Flare up like a flame
and make big shadows I can move in.

Let everything happen to you: beauty and terror.
Just keep going. No feeling is final.
Don't let yourself lose me.

Nearby is the country they call life.
You will know it by its seriousness.

Give me your hand.

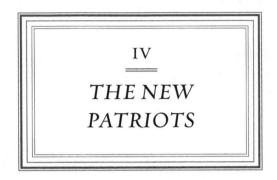

IV

THE NEW
PATRIOTS

It is a sign of great inner insecurity to be hostile to the unfamiliar.

—ANAÏS NIN

Praise Song for the Day
Elizabeth Alexander

A Poem for Barack Obama's Presidential Inauguration

Each day we go about our business,
walking past each other, catching each other's
eyes or not, about to speak or speaking.

All about us is noise. All about us is
noise and bramble, thorn and din, each
one of our ancestors on our tongues.

Someone is stitching up a hem, darning
a hole in a uniform, patching a tire,
repairing the things in need of repair.

Someone is trying to make music somewhere,
with a pair of wooden spoons on an oil drum,
with cello, boom box, harmonica, voice.

A woman and her son wait for the bus.
A farmer considers the changing sky.
A teacher says, *Take out your pencils. Begin.*

We encounter each other in words, words
spiny or smooth, whispered or declaimed,
words to consider, reconsider.

We cross dirt roads and highways that mark
the will of some one and then others, who said
I need to see what's on the other side.

I know there's something better down the road.
We need to find a place where we are safe.
We walk into that which we cannot yet see.

Say it plain: that many have died for this day.
Sing the names of the dead who brought us here,
who laid the train tracks, raised the bridges,

picked the cotton and the lettuce, built
brick by brick the glittering edifices
they would then keep clean and work inside of.

Praise song for struggle, praise song for the day.
Praise song for every hand-lettered sign,
the figuring-it-out at kitchen tables.

Some live by *love thy neighbor as thyself,*
others by *first do no harm* or *take no more
than you need.* What if the mightiest word is love?

Love beyond marital, filial, national,
love that casts a widening pool of light,
love with no need to pre-empt grievance.

In today's sharp sparkle, this winter air,
any thing can be made, any sentence begun.
On the brink, on the brim, on the cusp,

praise song for walking forward in that light.

I would not have you descend into your own dream. I would have you be a conscious citizen of this terrible and beautiful world.

—TA-NEHISI COATES, *Between the World and Me*

I, Too

Langston Hughes

I, too, sing America.

I am the darker brother.
They send me to eat in the kitchen
When company comes,
But I laugh,
And eat well,
And grow strong.

Tomorrow,
I'll be at the table
When company comes.
Nobody'll dare
Say to me,
"Eat in the kitchen,"
Then.

Besides,
They'll see how beautiful I am
And be ashamed—

I, too, am America.

SOMEDAY I'LL LOVE OCEAN VUONG

Ocean Vuong

Ocean, don't be afraid.
The end of the road is so far ahead
it is already behind us.
Don't worry. Your father is only your father
until one of you forgets. Like how the spine
won't remember its wings
no matter how many times our knees
kiss the pavement. Ocean,
are you listening? The most beautiful part
of your body is wherever
your mother's shadow falls.
Here's the house with childhood
whittled down to a single red tripwire.
Don't worry. Just call it *horizon*
& you'll never reach it.
Here's today. Jump. I promise it's not
a lifeboat. Here's the man
whose arms are wide enough to gather
your leaving. & here the moment,
just after the lights go out, when you can still see
the faint torch between his legs.
How you use it again & again
to find your own hands.
You asked for a second chance
& are given a mouth to empty into.
Don't be afraid, the gunfire
is only the sound of people
trying to live a little longer. Ocean. Ocean,

get up. The most beautiful part of your body
is where it's headed. & remember,
loneliness is still time spent
with the world. Here's
the room with everyone in it.
Your dead friends passing
through you like wind
through a wind chime. Here's a desk
with the gimp leg & a brick
to make it last. Yes, here's a room
so warm & blood-close,
I swear, you will wake—
& mistake these walls
for skin.

I have seen greatness and power, wealth, prosperity and incomparable development. I was never sad that we are a small and unfinished part of the world. To be small, unsettled and uncompleted is a good and courageous mission.

—Karel Čapek

SECOND ATTEMPT CROSSING
Javier Zamora
FOR CHINO

In the middle of that desert that didn't look like sand
    and sand only,
in the middle of those acacias, whiptails, and coyotes, someone
    yelled "¡La Migra!" and everyone ran.
In that dried creek where 40 of us slept, we turned to each other
    and you flew from my side in the dirt.

Black-throated sparrows and dawn
    hitting the tops of mesquites,
beautifully. Against the herd of legs,

    you sprinted back toward me,
I jumped on your shoulders,
    and we ran from the white trucks. It was then the gun
ready to press its index.

    I said, "freeze, Chino, ¡pará por favor!"

So I wouldn't touch their legs that kicked you,
    you pushed me under your chest,
and I've never thanked you.

Beautiful *Chino*—

the only name I know to call you by—
    farewell your tattooed chest:

the M, the S, the 13. Farewell
    the phone number you gave me
when you went east to Virginia,
    and I went west to San Francisco.

You called twice a month,
    then your cousin said the gang you ran from
in San Salvador
    found you in Alexandria. Farewell
your brown arms that shielded me then,
    that shield me now, from La Migra.

Now That We Have Tasted Hope
Khaled Mattawa

Now that we have come out of hiding,
Why would we live again in the tombs we'd made out of our
   souls?

And the sundered bodies that we've reassembled
With prayers and consolations,
What would their torn parts be, other than flesh?

Now that we have tasted hope
And dressed each other's wounds with the legends of our
   oneness
Would we not prefer to close our mouths forever shut
On the wine that swilled inside them?

Having dreamed the same dream,
Having found the water behind a thousand mirages,
Why would we hide from the sun again
Or fear the night sky after we've reached the ends of darkness,
Live in death again after all the life our dead have given us?

Listen to me Zow'ya, Beida, Ajdabya, Tobruk, Nalut,
Listen to me Derna, Musrata, Benghazi, Zintan,
Listen to me houses, alleys, courtyards, and streets that throng
   my veins,
Some day soon, in your freed light, in the shade of your proud
   trees,

Your excavated heroes will return to their thrones in your
    martyrs' squares,
Lovers will hold each other's hands.

I need not look far to imagine the nerves dying,
Rejecting the life that blood sends them.
I need not look deep into my past to seek a thousand hopeless
    vistas.
But now that I have tasted hope
I have fallen into the embrace of my own rugged innocence.

How long were my ancient days?
I no longer care to count.
I no longer care to measure.
How bitter was the bread of bitterness?
I no longer care to recall.

Now that we have tasted hope, this hard-earned crust,
We would sooner die than seek any other taste to life,
Any other way of being human.

ABEYANCE

Rebecca Foust

LETTER TO MY TRANSGENDER DAUGHTER

I made soup tonight, with cabbage, chard
and thyme picked outside our back door.
For this moment the room is warm and light,
and I can presume you safe somewhere.
I know the night lives inside you. I know grave,
sad errors were made, dividing you, and hiding
you from you inside. I know a girl like you
was knifed last week, another set aflame.
I know I lack the words, or all the words I say
are wrong. I know I'll call and you won't answer,
and still I'll call. I want to tell you
you were loved with all I had, recklessly,
and with abandon, loved the way the cabbage
in my garden near-inverts itself, splayed
to catch each last ray of sun. And how
the feeling furling-in only makes the heart
more dense and green. Tonight it seems like
something one could bear.

Guess what, Dad and I finally figured out Pandora,
and after all those years of silence, our old music
fills the air. It fills the air, and somehow, here,
at this instant and for this instant only
—perhaps three bars—what I recall
equals all I feel, and I remember all the words.

do you know what it's like to live
someplace that loves you back?

—Danez Smith, from
"summer, somewhere"

WHAT CHANGES
Naomi Shihab Nye

My father's hopes travel with me
years after he died. Someday
we will learn how to live. All of us
surviving without violence
never stop dreaming how to cure it.
What changes? Crossing a small street
in Doha Souk, nut shops shuttered,
a handkerchief lies crumpled in the street,
maroon and white, like one my father had,
from Jordan. Perfectly placed
in his pocket under his smile, for years.
He would have given it to anyone.
How do we continue all these days?

To Be a Woman

Alice Walker

To be a woman
Does not mean
To Wear
A shroud;

The feminine
Is not
Dead
Nor is she
Sleeping

Angry, yes,
Seething, yes.

Biding her time;

Yes.

Yes.

DEAR WHITE AMERICA

Danez Smith

WITH LINES FROM AMIRI BARAKA AND JAMES BALDWIN

I have left Earth in search of darker planets, a solar system that revolves too near a black hole. I have left a patch of dirt in my place & many of you won't know the difference; we are indeed the same color, one of us would eventually become the other. You may give it my name if it makes you feel better while running your hands through its soiled scalp. I have left Earth in search of a new God. I do not trust the God you have given us. My grandmother's hallelujah is only outdone by the fear she nurses every time the blood-fat summer swallows another child who used to sing in the choir. Take your God back. Though his songs are beautiful, his miracles are inconsistent. I want the fate of Lazarus for Renisha, I want Chucky, Bo, Meech, Trayvon, Sean & Jonylah risen three days after their entombing, their ghost re-gifted flesh & blood, their flesh & blood re-gifted their children. I have left Earth, I am equal parts sick of your 'go back to Africa' as I am your 'I just don't see color' (neither did the poplar tree). We did not build your boats (though we did leave a trail of kin to guide us home). We did not build your prisons (though we did & we fill them too). We did not ask to be part of your America (though are we not America? Her joints brittle & dragging a ripped gown through Oakland?). I can't stand your ground. I am sick of calling your recklessness the law. Each night, I count my brothers. & in the morning, when some do not survive to be counted, I count the holes they leave. I reach for black folks & touch only air. Your master magic trick, America. Now he's breathing, now he don't. Abra-cadaver. White bread voodoo. This systemic sorcery you claim not to practice, but have no problem benefitting from. I tried, white people. I tried to love you, but you spent my brother's funeral making plans for brunch, talking too loud next to his bones. You interrupted my black veiled mourning with some mess about an article you read on Buzzfeed. You took one look at the river, plump with the body of boy after boy after boy & asked 'why does it always have to be about race?' Because you made it so! Because you put an asterisk on my sister's gorgeous face! Because you call her pretty (for a black girl)! Because black girls go missing without so much as a whisper of where?! Because there is no Amber Alert for the Amber Skinned Girls! Because our heroes always end up shot or shootin-up! Because we didn't invent the bullet! Because crack was not our recipe! Because Jordan boomed. Because Emmitt whistled. Because Huey P. spoke. Because Martin preached. Because black boys can always be too loud to live. Because this land is scared of the Black mind. Because they have sold the Black body & appropriated Soul. Because it's taken my father's time, my mother's time, my uncle's time, my brother's & my sister's time, my niece's & my nephew's time . . . how much time do you want for your progress? I have left Earth to find a land where my kin can be safe. I will not rest until black people ain't but people the same color as the good, wet earth, until that means something, until our existence isn't up for debate, until it is honored & blessed & loved & left alone, until then I bid you well, I bid you war, I bid you our lives to gamble with no more. I have left Earth & I am touching everything you beg your telescopes to show you. I am giving the stars their right names. & this life, this new story & history you cannot steal or sell or cast overboard or hang or beat or drown or own or redline or shot or shackle or silence or impoverish choke or lock up or cover up or bury or ruin

    This, if only this one, is ours.

FROM
"DAILY BREAD"

Ocean Vuong

Listen,
the year is gone. I know
nothing of my country. I write things
down. I build a life & tear it apart
& the sun keeps shining.

Refugees

Brian Bilston

They have no need of our help
So do not tell me
These haggard faces could belong to you or me
Should life have dealt a different hand
We need to see them for who they really are
Chancers and scroungers
Layabouts and loungers
With bombs up their sleeves
Cut-throats and thieves
They are not
Welcome here
We should make them
Go back to where they came from
They cannot
Share our food
Share our homes
Share our countries
Instead let us
Build a wall to keep them out
It is not okay to say
These are people just like us
A place should only belong to those who are born there
Do not be so stupid to think that
The world can be looked at another way

(now read from bottom to top)

@ the Crossroads—
A Sudden American Poem

Juan Felipe Herrera

RIP Philando Castile, Alton Sterling, Dallas police
officers Lorne Ahrens, Michael Krol, Michael J.
Smith, Brent Thompson, and Patrick Zamarripa—
and all their families. And to all those injured.

                              Let us celebrate the lives of all
As we reflect & pray & meditate on their brutal deaths
Let us celebrate those who marched at night who spoke of peace
& chanted Black Lives Matter
Let us celebrate the officers dressed in Blues ready to protect
Let us know the departed as we did not know them before—
    their faces,
Bodies, names—what they loved, their words, the stories they
    often spoke
Before we return to the usual business of our days, let us know
    their lives intimately
Let us take this moment & impossible as this may sound—let us
    find
The beauty in their lives in the midst of their sudden & never
    imagined vanishing

Let us consider the Dallas shooter—what made him
                              what happened in
                                 Afghanistan
                what
        flames burned inside

(Who was that man in Baton Rouge with a red shirt selling CDs
    in the parking lot
Who was that man in Minnesota toppled on the car seat with a
    perforated arm
& a continent-shaped flood of blood on his white T who was
That man prone & gone by the night pillar of El Centro College
    in Dallas)

This could be the first step
        in the new evaluation of our society   This could be
        the first step of all of our lives

A Queerification

Regie Cabico

—FOR CREATIVITY AND CRISIS AT THE NATIONAL MALL

queer me
shift me
transgress me
tell my students i'm gay
tell chick fil a i'm queer
tell the new york times i'm straight
tell the mail man i'm a lesbian
tell american airlines
i don't know what my gender is
like me
liking you
like summer blockbuster armrest dates
armrest cinematic love
elbow to forearm in the dark
humor me queerly
fill me with laughter
make me high with queer gas
decompress me from centuries of spanish inquisition
& self-righteous judgment
like the blood my blood
that has mixed w/ the colonizer
& the colonized
in the extinct & instinct to love
bust memories of water & heat
& hot & breath
beating skin on skin fluttering

bruise me into vapors
bleed me into air
fly me over sub-saharan africa & asia & antarctica
explode me from the closet of my fears
graffiti me out of doubt
bend me like bamboo
propose to me
divorce me
divide me into your spirit 2 spirit half spirit
& shadow me w/ fluttering tongues
& caresses beyond head
heart chakras
fist smashing djembes
between my hesitations
haiku me into 17 bursts of blossoms & cold saki
de-ethnicize me
de-clothe me
de-gender me in brassieres
& prosthetic genitalias
burn me on a brazier
wearing a brassiere
in bitch braggadocio soprano bass
magnificat me in vespers
of hallelujah & amen
libate me in halos
heal me in halls of femmy troubadors
announcing my hiv status
or your status
i am not afraid to love you
implant dialects as if they were lilacs
in my ear

medicate me with a lick & a like
i am not afraid to love you
so demand me
reclaim me
queerify me

I have met brave women who are exploring the outer edge of human possibility, with no history to guide them, and with a courage to make themselves vulnerable that I find moving beyond words.

—GLORIA STEINEM

The Border: A Double Sonnet

Alberto Ríos

The border is a line that birds cannot see.
The border is a beautiful piece of paper folded carelessly in half.
The border is where flint first met steel, starting a century of
fires.
The border is a belt that is too tight, holding things up but
making it hard to breathe.
The border is a rusted hinge that does not bend.
The border is the blood clot in the river's vein.
The border says *stop* to the wind, but the wind speaks another
language, and keeps going.
The border is a brand, the "Double-X" of barbed wire scarred
into the skin of so many.
The border has always been a welcome stopping place but is now
a stop sign, always red.
The border is a jump rope still there even after the game is
finished.
The border is a real crack in an imaginary dam.
The border used to be an actual place, but now, it is the act of a
thousand imaginations.
The border, the word *border,* sounds like *order,* but in this place
they do not rhyme.
The border is a handshake that becomes a squeezing contest.

The border smells like cars at noon and wood smoke in the
evening.
The border is the place between the two pages in a book where
the spine is bent too far.
The border is two men in love with the same woman.

The border is an equation in search of an equals sign.

The border is the location of the factory where lightning and thunder are made.

The border is "NoNo" The Clown, who can't make anyone laugh.

The border is a locked door that has been promoted.

The border is a moat but without a castle on either side.

The border has become Checkpoint *Chale*.

The border is a place of plans constantly broken and repaired and broken.

The border is mighty, but even the parting of the seas created a path, not a barrier.

The border is a big, neat, clean, clear black line on a map that does not exist.

The border is the line in new bifocals: below, small things get bigger; above, nothing changes.

The border is a skunk with a white line down its back.

You're Dead, America
Danez Smith

i fed your body to the fish
traded it at lunch for milk

i know where they buried you
cause it's my mouth

they tell me *bootstraps*
& i spit up a little leather

they tell me *Christ*
but you don't have black friends

during the anthem
i hum *Niggas in Paris*

i cha cha slide over the flag
C-walk on occasion

i put a spell on you
it called for 3/5s of my blood

apple pie, red
bones & a full moon

but instead i did it
in the daylight, wanting you

to see me ending you
stupid stupid me

i know better than to fuck
with a recipe

i don't make chicken
when I don't have eggs

look at what i did: on the TV
the man from TV

is gonna be president
he has no words

& hair beyond simile
you're dead, America

& where you died
grew something worse—

crop white as the smile
of a man with his country on his side

a gun on his other side

//

tomorrow, i'll have hope.

tomorrow i can shift the wreckage

& find a seed.

i don't know what will grow

i've lost my faith in this garden

the bees are dying

the water poisons whole cities

but my honeyed kin

those brown folks who make

up the nation of my heart

only allegiance i stand for

realer than any god

for them i bury whatever

this country thought it was.

What didn't you do to bury me
But you forgot that I was a seed.

—DINOS CHRISTIANOPOULOS

"AMERICA, AMERICA"
Saadi Youssef

God save America,
  My home, sweet home!

We are not hostages, America,
and your soldiers are not God's soldiers . . .
We are the poor ones, ours is the earth of the drowned gods,
the gods of bulls,
the gods of fires,
the gods of sorrows that intertwine clay and blood in a song . . .
We are the poor, ours is the god of the poor,
who emerges out of farmers' ribs,
hungry
and bright,
and raises heads up high . . .

America, we are the dead.
Let your soldiers come.
Whoever kills a man, let him resurrect him.
We are the drowned ones, dear lady.
We are the drowned.
Let the water come.

KINDNESS
Naomi Shihab Nye

Before you know what kindness really is
you must lose things,
feel the future dissolve in a moment
like salt in a weakened broth.
What you held in your hand,
what you counted and carefully saved,
all this must go so you know
how desolate the landscape can be
between the regions of kindness.
How you ride and ride
thinking the bus will never stop,
the passengers eating maize and chicken
will stare out the window forever.

Before you learn the tender gravity of kindness
you must travel where the Indian in a white poncho
lies dead by the side of the road.
You must see how this could be you,
how he too was someone
who journeyed through the night with plans
and the simple breath that kept him alive.

Before you know kindness as the deepest thing inside,
you must know sorrow as the other deepest thing.
You must wake up with sorrow.
You must speak to it till your voice
catches the thread of all sorrows
and you see the size of the cloth.

Then it is only kindness that makes sense anymore,
only kindness that ties your shoes
and sends you out into the day to gaze at bread,
only kindness that raises its head
from the crowd of the world to say
It is I you have been looking for,
and then goes with you everywhere
like a shadow or a friend.

MOON FOR OUR DAUGHTERS

Annie Finch

Moon that is linking our daughters'
Choices, and still more beginnings,
Threaded alive with our shadows,

These are our bodies' own voices,
Powers of each of our bodies,
Threading, unbroken, begetting

Flowers from each of our bodies.
These are our spiraling borders
Carrying on your beginnings,

Chaining through shadows to daughters,
Moving beyond our beginnings,
Moon of our daughters, and mothers.

LANGSTON HUGHES
Gwendolyn Brooks

Langston Hughes
is merry glory
Is saltatory.
Yet grips his right of twisting free.
Has a long reach,
Strong speech,
Remedial fears,
Muscular tears.
Holds horticulture
In the eye of the vulture
Infirm profession.
In the Compression—
In mud and blood and sudden death—
In the breath
Of the holocaust he
Is helmsman, hatchet, headlight.
See
One restless in the exotic time! and ever,
Till the air is cured of its fever.

THE NEW COLOSSUS

Emma Lazarus

Not like the brazen giant of Greek fame,
With conquering limbs astride from land to land;
Here at our sea-washed, sunset gates shall stand
A mighty woman with a torch, whose flame
Is the imprisoned lightning, and her name
Mother of Exiles. From her beacon-hand
Glows world-wide welcome; her mild eyes command
The air-bridged harbor that twin cities frame.
"Keep, ancient lands, your storied pomp!" cries she
With silent lips. "Give me your tired, your poor,
Your huddled masses yearning to breathe free,
The wretched refuse of your teeming shore.
Send these, the homeless, tempest-tost to me,
I lift my lamp beside the golden door!"

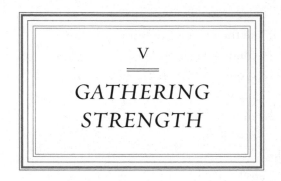

V

GATHERING
STRENGTH

Be patient and tough; one day this pain will be useful to you.

—Ovid

WHEN I RISE UP

Georgia Douglas Johnson

When I rise up above the earth,
And look down on the things that fetter me,
I beat my wings upon the air,
Or tranquil lie,
Surge after surge of potent strength
Like incense comes to me
When I rise up above the earth
And look down upon the things that fetter me.

I HAVE NO QUARREL WITH YOU
Florence Brooks Whitehouse

I have no quarrel with you; but I stand
For the clear right to hold my life my own;
The clean, clear right. To mould it as I will,
Not as you will, with or apart from you;
To make of it a thing of brain and blood,
Of tangible substance and of turbulent thought.
No thin gray shadow of the life of man.
Your love, perchance, may set a crown upon it;
But I may crown myself in other ways.
As you have done who are one flesh with me.
I have no quarrel with you—but henceforth,
This you must know; the world is mine, as yours,
The pulsing strength and passion and heart of it;
The work I set my hand to, women's work,
Because I set my hand to it.

SQUALL

Leonora Speyer

The squall sweeps gray-winged across the obliterated hills,
And the startled lake seems to run before it;
From the wood comes a clamor of leaves,
Tugging at the twigs,
Pouring from the branches,
And suddenly the birds are still.

Thunder crumples the sky,
Lightning tears at it.

And now the rain!
The rain—thudding—implacable—
The wind, reveling in the confusion of great pines!

And a silver sifting of light,
A coolness;
A sense of summer anger passing,
Of summer gentleness creeping nearer—
Penitent, tearful,
Forgiven!

Difficulties break some men but make others. No axe is sharp enough to cut the soul of a sinner who keeps on trying, one armed with the hope that he will rise even in the end.

—NELSON MANDELA, letter to WINNIE MANDELA,
February 1, 1975, written on Robben Island

Be like the headline against which the waves break and break: it stands firm, until presently the watery tumult around it subsides once more to rest. "How unlucky I am, that this should have happened to me!" By no means; say rather, "How lucky I am, that it has left me with no bitterness; unshaken by the present, and undismayed by the future." The thing could have happened to anyone, but not everyone would have emerged unembittered. So why put the one down to misfortune, rather than the other to good fortune? Can a man call anything at all a misfortune, if it is not a contravention of his nature; and can it be a contravention of his nature if it is not against that nature's will? Well, then: you have learnt to know that will. Does this thing which has happened hinder you from being just, magnanimous, temperate, judicious, discreet, truthful, self-respecting, independent, and all else by which a man's nature comes to its fulfillment? So here is a rule to remember in future, when anything tempts you to feel bitter: not, "This is a misfortune," but "To bear this worthily is good fortune."

—MARCUS AURELIUS, *Meditations*

STILL I RISE
Maya Angelou

You may write me down in history
With your bitter, twisted lies,
You may trod me in the very dirt
But still, like dust, I'll rise.

Does my sassiness upset you?
Why are you beset with gloom?
'Cause I walk like I've got oil wells
Pumping in my living room.

Just like moons and like suns,
With the certainty of tides,
Just like hopes springing high,
Still I'll rise.

Did you want to see me broken?
Bowed head and lowered eyes?
Shoulders falling down like teardrops,
Weakened by my soulful cries?

Does my haughtiness offend you?
Don't you take it awful hard
'Cause I laugh like I've got gold mines
Diggin' in my own backyard.

You may shoot me with your words,
You may cut me with your eyes,

You may kill me with your hatefulness,
But still, like air, I'll rise.

Does my sexiness upset you?
Does it come as a surprise
That I dance like I've got diamonds
At the meeting of my thighs?

Out of the huts of history's shame
I rise
Up from a past that's rooted in pain
I rise
I'm a black ocean, leaping and wide,
Welling and swelling I bear in the tide.

Leaving behind nights of terror and fear
I rise
Into a daybreak that's wondrously clear
I rise
Bringing the gifts that my ancestors gave,
I am the dream and the hope of the slave.
I rise
I rise
I rise.

I often think that the night is more alive and more richly colored than the day.

—VINCENT VAN GOGH

The Peace of Wild Things

Wendell Berry

When despair grows in me
and I wake in the night at the least sound
in fear of what my life and my children's lives may be,
I go and lie down where the wood drake
rests in his beauty on the water, and the great heron feeds.
I come into the peace of wild things
who do not tax their lives with forethought
of grief. I come into the presence of still water.
And I feel above me the day-blind stars
waiting for their light. For a time
I rest in the grace of the world, and am free.

EVERYBODY HAS A HEARTACHE, A BLUES
Joy Harjo

In the United Terminal in Chicago at five on a Friday afternoon
The sky is breaking with rain and wind and all the flights
Are delayed forever. We will never get to where we are going
And there's no way back to where we've been.
The sun and the moon have disappeared to an island far from
  anywhere.

Everybody has a heartache—

The immense gatekeeper of Gate Z-100 keeps his cool.
This guardian of the sky teases me and makes me smile through
  the mess,
Building up his airline by stacking it against the company I
  usually travel:
Come on over to our side, we'll treat you nice.
I laugh as he hands me back my ticket, then he turns to charm
The next customer, his feet tired in his minimum wage shoes.

Everybody has a heartache—

Everyone's eating fried, sweet, soft and fat,
While we wait for word in the heart of the scrambled beast.
The sparkle of soda wets the dream core.
That woman over there the color of broth, did what she was
  told.
It's worked out well as can be expected in a world
Where she was no beauty queen and was never seen,
Always in the back of someplace in the back—

She holds the newest baby. He has the croup.
Shush, shush. Go to sleep, my little baby sheepie.
He sits up front of her with his new crop of teeth.

Everybody has a heartache—

The man with his head bobbing to music no one else can hear,
    speaks to no one, but his body does.
Half his liver is swollen with anger; the other half is trying
To apologize—
What a mess I've made of history, he thinks without thinking.
Mother coming through the screen door, her clothes torn,
Whimpering: *it's okay baby, please don't cry.*
Don't cry. Baby don't cry.
And he never cries again.

Everybody has a heartache—

Baby girl dressed to impress, toddles about with lace on this and
    ruffle on that—
Her mother's relatives are a few hundred miles away poised to
    welcome.
They might as well live on a planet of ice cream.
She's a brand new wing, grown up from a family's broken hope.
Dance girl, you carry our joy.
Just don't look down.

Everybody has a heartache—

Good-looking punk girl taps this on her screen
to a stranger she has never seen:

Just before dawn, you're high again beneath a breaking sky,
I was slick fine leather with a drink in my hand.
Flying with a comet messenger nobody sees.
The quick visitor predicts that the top will be the bottom
And the bottom will flatten and dive into the sea.

I want to tell her:
You will dine with the lobster king, and
You will dance with crabs clicking castanets. You will sleep
Walk beyond the vestibule of sadness with a stranger
You have loved for years.

Everybody has a heartache—

This silence in the noise of the terminal is a mountain of bison
  skulls.
Nobody knows, nobody sees—
Unless the indigenous are dancing powwow all decked out in
  flash and beauty
We just don't exist. We've been dispersed to an outlaw cowboy
  tale.
What were they thinking with all those guns and those handcuffs
In a size for babies?
They just don't choose to remember.
We're here.

In the terminal of stopped time I went unsteady to the beat,
Driven by a hungry spirit who is drunk with words and songs.
What can I do?
I have to take care of it.
The famished spirit eats fire, poetry and pain; it only wants love.

I argue:

You want love?
Do you even know what it looks like, smells like?

But you cannot argue with hungry spirits.

Everybody has a heartache—

I don't know exactly where I'm going; I only know where I've
    been,
I want to tell the man who sifted through the wreck to find us
In the blues shack of disappeared history—
I feel the weight of his heart against my cheek.
His hand is on my back pulling me to him in the dark, to a place
No soldiers can reach—

No matter fire leaping through holes in jump time,
No matter earthquake, or the breaking of love spilling over the
    drek of matter
In the ether, stacking one burden
Against the other—

We will all find our way.

We have a heartache.

One always begins to forgive a place as soon as it's left behind.

—CHARLES DICKENS

LINES FOR WINTER
Mark Strand

FOR ROS KRAUSS

Tell yourself
as it gets cold and gray falls from the air
that you will go on
walking, hearing
the same tune no matter where
you find yourself—
inside the dome of dark
or under the cracking white
of the moon's gaze in a valley of snow.
Tonight as it gets cold
tell yourself
what you know which is nothing
but the tune your bones play
as you keep going. And you will be able
for once to lie down under the small fire
of winter stars.
And if it happens that you cannot
go on or turn back
and you find yourself
where you will be at the end,
tell yourself
in that final flowing of cold through your limbs
that you love what you are.

INVICTUS
William Ernest Henley

Out of the night that covers me,
Black as the pit from pole to pole,
I thank whatever gods may be
For my unconquerable soul.

In the fell clutch of circumstance
I have not winced nor cried aloud.
Under the bludgeonings of chance
My head is bloody, but unbowed.

Beyond this place of wrath and tears
Looms but the Horror of the shade,
And yet the menace of the years
Finds and shall find me unafraid.

It matters not how strait the gate,
How charged with punishments the scroll,
I am the master of my fate,
I am the captain of my soul.

The Gift to Sing

James Weldon Johnson

Sometimes the mist overhangs my path,
And blackening clouds about me cling;
But, oh, I have a magic way
To turn the gloom to cheerful day—
    I softly sing.

And if the way grows darker still,
Shadowed by Sorrow's somber wing,
With glad defiance in my throat,
I pierce the darkness with a note,
    And sing, and sing.

I brood not over the broken past,
Nor dread whatever time may bring;
No nights are dark, no days are long,
While in my heart there swells a song,
    And I can sing.

When you know better, you do better.

—MAYA ANGELOU

BE NOBODY'S DARLING
Alice Walker

Be nobody's darling;
Be an outcast.
Take the contradictions
Of your life
And wrap around
You like a shawl,
To parry stones
To keep you warm.

Watch the people succumb
To madness
With ample cheer;
Let them look askance at you
And you askance reply.

Be an outcast;
Be pleased to walk alone
(Uncool)
Or line the crowded
River beds
With other impetuous
Fools.

Make a merry gathering
On the bank
Where thousands perished
For brave hurt words
They said.

Be nobody's darling;
Be an outcast.
Qualified to live
Among your dead.

CHEERFULNESS TAUGHT BY REASON

Elizabeth Barrett Browning

I think we are too ready with complaint
In this fair world of God's. Had we no hope
Indeed beyond the zenith and the slope
Of yon gray blank of sky, we might be faint
To muse upon eternity's constraint
Round our aspirant souls. But since the scope
Must widen early, is it well to droop,
For a few days consumed in loss and taint?
O pusillanimous Heart, be comforted,—
And, like a cheerful traveller, take the road—
Singing beside the hedge. What if the bread
Be bitter in thine inn, and thou unshod
To meet the flints?—At least it may be said,
"Because the way is short, I thank thee, God!"

A DREAM WITHIN A DREAM

Edgar Allan Poe

Take this kiss upon the brow!
And, in parting from you now,
Thus much let me avow—
You are not wrong, who deem
That my days have been a dream;
Yet if hope has flown away
In a night, or in a day,
In a vision, or in none,
Is it therefore the less *gone*?
All that we see or seem
Is but a dream within a dream.

I stand amid the roar
Of a surf-tormented shore,
And I hold within my hand
Grains of the golden sand—
How few! yet how they creep
Through my fingers to the deep,
While I weep—while I weep!
O God! can I not grasp
Them with a tighter clasp?
O God! can I not save
One from the pitiless wave?
Is *all* that we see or seem
But a dream within a dream?

When you come to one of the many moments in life when you must give an account of yourself, provide a ledger of what you have been, and done, and meant to the world, do not, I pray, discount that you filled a dying man's days with a sated joy, a joy unknown to me in all my prior years, a joy that does not hunger for more and more, but rests, satisfied. In this time, right now, that is an enormous thing.

—PAUL KALANITHI, *When Breath Becomes Air*

Song of Quietness
Robinson Jeffers

Drink deep, drink deep of quietness,
And on the margins of the sea
Remember not thine old distress
Nor all the miseries to be.
Calmer than mists, and cold
As they, that fold on fold
Up the dim valley are rolled,
Learn thou to be.

The Past—it was a feverish dream,
A drunken slumber full of tears.
The Future—O what wild wings gleam,
Wheeled in the van of desperate years!
Thou lovedst the evening: dawn
Glimmers; the night is gone:—
What dangers lure thee on,
What dreams more fierce?

But meanwhile, now the east is gray,
The hour is pale, the cocks yet dumb,
Be glad before the birth of day,
Take thy brief rest ere morning come:
Here in the beautiful woods
All night the sea-mist floods,—
Thy last of solitudes,
Thy yearlong home.

LOVE
William Carlos Williams

Love is twain, it is not single,
Gold and silver mixed to one,
Passion 'tis and pain which mingle
Glist'ring then for aye undone.

Pain it is not; wondering pity
Dies or e'er the pang is fled;
Passion 'tis not, foul and gritty,
Born one instant, instant dead.

Love is twain, it is not single,
Gold and silver mixed to one,
Passion 'tis and pain which mingle
Glist'ring then for aye undone.

The Day Is Done

Henry Wadsworth Longfellow

The day is done, and the darkness
    Falls from the wings of Night,
As a feather is wafted downward
    From an eagle in his flight.

I see the lights of the village
    Gleam through the rain and the mist,
And a feeling of sadness comes o'er me
    That my soul cannot resist:

A feeling of sadness and longing,
    That is not akin to pain,
And resembles sorrow only
    As the mist resembles the rain.

Come, read to me some poem,
    Some simple and heartfelt lay,
That shall soothe this restless feeling,
    And banish the thoughts of day.

Not from the grand old masters,
    Not from the bards sublime,
Whose distant footsteps echo
    Through the corridors of Time.

For, like strains of martial music,
    Their mighty thoughts suggest

Life's endless toil and endeavor;
        And to-night I long for rest.

Read from some humbler poet,
        Whose songs gushed from his heart,
As showers from the clouds of summer,
        Or tears from the eyelids start;

Who, through long days of labor,
        And nights devoid of ease,
Still heard in his soul the music
        Of wonderful melodies.

Such songs have power to quiet
        The restless pulse of care,
And come like the benediction
        That follows after prayer.

Then read from the treasured volume
        The poem of thy choice,
And lend to the rhyme of the poet
        The beauty of thy voice.

And the night shall be filled with music,
        And the cares, that infest the day,
Shall fold their tents, like the Arabs,
        And as silently steal away.

VI

TO SUMMON
HOPE

Whatever happens to you, you can either see it as a curse and suffer it, or you can see it as a blessing and make use of it.

—SADHGURU

Prayer at Sunrise
James Weldon Johnson

Now thou art risen, and thy day begun.
How shrink the shrouding mists before thy face,
As up thou spring'st to thy diurnal race!
How darkness chases darkness to the west,
As shades of light on light rise radiant from thy crest!
For thee, great source of strength, emblem of might,
In hours of darkest gloom there is no night.
Thou shinest on though clouds hide thee from sight,
And through each break thou sendest down thy light.

O greater Maker of this Thy great sun,
Give me the strength this one day's race to run,
Fill me with light, fill me with sun-like strength,
Fill me with joy to rob the day its length.
Light from within, light that will outward shine,
Strength to make strong some weaker heart than mine,
Joy to make glad each soul that feels its touch;
Great Father of the sun, I ask this much.

Where the Mind Is Without Fear
Rabindranath Tagore

Where the mind is without fear and the head is held high
Where knowledge is free
Where the world has not been broken up into fragments
By narrow domestic walls
Where words come out from the depth of truth
Where tireless striving stretches its arms towards perfection
Where the clear stream of reason has not lost its way
Into the dreary desert sand of dead habit
Where the mind is led forward by thee
Into ever-widening thought and action
Into that heaven of freedom, my Father, let my country awake.

For we are like olives: only when we are crushed do we yield what is best in us.

—BOHUMIL HRABAL, *Too Loud a Solitude*

"Hope" is the thing with feathers
Emily Dickinson

"Hope" is the thing with feathers—
That perches in the soul—
And sings the tune without the words—
And never stops—at all—

And sweetest—in the Gale—is heard—
And sore must be the storm—
That could abash the little Bird
That kept so many warm—

I've heard it in the chillest land—
And on the strangest Sea—
Yet—never—in Extremity,
It asked a crumb—of me.

Clouds come floating into my life, no longer to carry
rain or usher storm, but to add color to my sunset sky.

—Rabindranath Tagore

I AM RUNNING INTO A NEW YEAR

Lucille Clifton

i am running into a new year
and the old years blow back
like a wind
that i catch in my hair
like strong fingers like
all my old promises and
it will be hard to let go
of what i said to myself
about myself
when i was sixteen and
twentysix and thirtysix
even thirtysix but
i am running into a new year
and i beg what i love and
i leave to forgive me

Our True Heritage

Thich Nhat Hanh

The cosmos is filled with precious gems.
I want to offer a handful of them to you this morning.
Each moment you are alive is a gem,
shining through and containing earth and sky,
water and clouds.

It needs you to breathe gently
for the miracles to be displayed.
Suddenly you hear the birds singing,
the pines chanting,
see the flowers blooming,
the blue sky,
the white clouds,
the smile and the marvelous look
of your beloved.

You, the richest person on Earth,
who have been going around begging for a living,
stop being the destitute child.
Come back and claim your heritage.
We should enjoy our happiness
and offer it to everyone.
Cherish this very moment.
Let go of the stream of distress
and embrace life fully in your arms.

You can cut all the flowers but you cannot keep Spring from coming.

—Pablo Neruda

From Blossoms

Li-Young Lee

From blossoms comes
this brown paper bag of peaches
we bought from the boy
at the bend in the road where we turned toward
signs painted *Peaches.*

From laden boughs, from hands,
from sweet fellowship in the bins,
comes nectar at the roadside, succulent
peaches we devour, dusty skin and all,
comes the familiar dust of summer, dust we eat.

O, to take what we love inside,
to carry within us an orchard, to eat
not only the skin, but the shade,
not only the sugar, but the days, to hold
the fruit in our hands, adore it, then bite into
the round jubilance of peach.

There are days we live
as if death were nowhere
in the background; from joy
to joy to joy, from wing to wing,
from blossom to blossom to
impossible blossom, to sweet impossible blossom.

Our greatest weakness lies in giving up. The most certain way to succeed is always to try just one more time.

—Thomas A. Edison

E. E. Cummings

i carry your heart with me(i carry it in
my heart)i am never without it(anywhere
i go you go,my dear;and whatever is done
by only me is your doing,my darling)
                    i fear
no fate(for you are my fate,my sweet)i want
no world(for beautiful you are my world,my true)
and it's you are whatever a moon has always meant
and whatever a sun will always sing is you

here is the deepest secret nobody knows
(here is the root of the root and the bud of the bud
and the sky of the sky of a tree called life;which grows
higher than the soul can hope or mind can hide)
and this is the wonder that's keeping the stars apart

i carry your heart(i carry it in my heart)

FOR THE NEW YEAR, 1981
Denise Levertov

I have a small grain of hope—
one small crystal that gleams
clear colors out of transparency.

I need more.

I break off a fragment
to send you.

Please take
this grain of a grain of hope
so that mine won't shrink.

Please share your fragment
so that yours will grow.

Only so, by division,
will hope increase,

like a clump of irises, which will cease to flower
unless you distribute
the clustered roots, unlikely source—
clumsy and earth-covered—
of grace.

BARTER

Sara Teasdale

Life has loveliness to sell,
All beautiful and splendid things,
Blue waves whitened on a cliff,
Soaring fire that sways and sings,
And children's faces looking up
Holding wonder like a cup.

Life has loveliness to sell,
Music like a curve of gold,
Scent of pine trees in the rain,
Eyes that love you, arms that hold,
And for your spirit's still delight,
Holy thoughts that star the night.

Spend all you have for loveliness,
Buy it and never count the cost;
For one white singing hour of peace
Count many a year of strife well lost,
And for a breath of ecstasy
Give all you have been, or could be.

There is a crack in everything.
That's how the light gets in.

—Leonard Cohen

Always There Are the Children
Nikki Giovanni

and always there are the children

there will be children in the heat of day
there will be children in the cold of winter

children like a quilted blanket
are welcomed in our old age

children like a block of ice to a desert sheik
are signs of status in our youth

we feed the children with our culture
that they might understand our travail

we nourish the children on our gods
that they may understand respect

we urge the children on the tracks
that our race will not fall short

but our children are not ours
nor we theirs they are future we are past

how do we welcome the future
not with the colonialism of the past
for that is our problem
not with the racism of the past
for that is their problem

not with the fears of our own status
for history is lived not dictated

we welcome the young of all groups
as our own with the solid nourishment
of food and warmth

we prepare the way with the solid
nourishment of self-actualization

we implore all the young to prepare for the young
because always there will be children

To be hopeful in bad times is not just foolishly romantic. It is based on the fact that human history is a history not only of cruelty, but also of compassion, sacrifice, courage, kindness. What we choose to emphasize in this complex history will determine our lives. If we see only the worst, it destroys our capacity to do something. If we remember those times and places—and there are so many—where people have behaved magnificently, this gives us the energy to act, and at least the possibility of sending this spinning top of a world in a different direction. And if we do act, in however small a way, we don't have to wait for some grand utopian future. The future is an infinite succession of presents, and to live now as we think human beings should live, in defiance of all that is bad around us, is itself a marvelous victory.

—HOWARD ZINN, *A Power Governments Cannot Suppress*

"In Memoriam, [Ring out, wild bells]"

Lord Alfred Tennyson

Ring out the old, ring in the new,
 Ring, happy bells, across the snow:
 The year is going, let him go;
Ring out the false, ring in the true.

ACKNOWLEDGMENTS

We would like to thank the many who have contributed suggestions of poems to include in this collection, including Lindsay Adkins, Jon Baker, Anna Bauer, Sarah Burnes, Kimberly Burns, Sheryl Cotleur, Camille Dewing-Vallejo, Benjamin Dreyer, Kristin Fassler, Sarah Feightner, Julie Grau, Emily Hartley, Ira Ken Lettrich, Victory Matsui, Katharine Blake McFarland, Whitney Peeling, Anna Pitoniak, Natasha Bronn Schrier, Polly Shulman, Cindy Spiegel, Anna Stoessinger, Michael Taeckens, David Ulin, and Laura van der Veer.

INDEX

PERMISSIONS ACKNOWLEDGMENTS

*Grateful acknowledgment is made to the following
for permission to reprint previously published material:*

ACADEMY OF AMERICAN POETS: "@ the Crossroads—A Sudden American Poem" by Juan Felipe Herrera originally published in the Academy of American Poets' Poem-a-Day series, July 10, 2016. Reprinted by permission of the Academy of American Poets, 75 Maiden Lane, Suite 901, New York, NY 10038, www.poets.org.

COLEMAN BARKS: "The Guest House" and "Out Beyond Ideas" by Rumi, translated by Coleman Barks. Reprinted by permission of Coleman Barks.

BROOKS PERMISSIONS: "Langston Hughes" by Gwendolyn Brooks. Reprinted by permission of Brooks Permissions.

BUZZFEED, INC.: "You're Dead, America" by Danez Smith. Reprinted by permission of Buzzfeed, Inc.

COPYRIGHT CLEARANCE CENTER ON BEHALF OF PRINCETON UNIVERSITY PRESS: "Four in the Morning" from *Sounds, Feelings, Thoughts: Seventy Poems* by Wisława Szymborska, translated and edited by Magnus J. Krynski and Robert A. Maguire, copyright © 1981 by Princeton University Press. Reprinted by permission of Copyright Clearance Center on behalf of Princeton University Press.

COUNTERPOINT: "The Peace of Wild Things" from *The Selected Poems of Wendell Berry*, copyright © 1998 by Wendell Berry. Reprinted by permission of *Counterpoint*.

FARRAR, STRAUS AND GIROUX: "Try to Praise the Mutilated World" from *Without End: New and Selected Poems* by Adam Zagajewski, translated by Clare Cavanagh, Renata Gorczynski, Benjamin Ivry, and C. K. Williams, copyright © 2002 by Adam Zagajewski, translation copyright © 2002 by Farrar, Straus and Giroux. Reprinted by permission of Farrar, Straus & Giroux.